PEACE O

The Christmas

David Boyle

Jointly published by Createspace and
THE REAL PRESS
www.therealpress.com

This edition published in 2015 by Createspace,
Originally published as an ebook by Endeavour Press in 2014
www.therealpress.com

© David Boyle

ISBN 978 1512270044

For my wonderful stepfather, Robert

"Yet with the woes of sin and strife
The world has suffered long;
Beneath the angel-strain have rolled
Two thousand years of wrong;
And man, at war with man, hears not
The love-song which they bring;
O hush the noise, ye men of strife,
And hear the angels sing.
It came upon a midnight clear', Edmund Sears, 1849

"For a single day, the opposing forces mingled in friendly conversation and even in games. It was an amazing spectacle, and must arouse bitter thoughts concerning those high-ranking conspirators against the peace of the world, who in their mad ambition had hounded such men on to take each other by the throat rather than by the hand."

Arthur Conan Doyle, *The British Campaign in France and Flanders 1914,* **1916**

"Dear Mother," wrote the nineteen-year-old future novelist Henry Williamson, serving with the London Rifle Brigade near Ploegsteert Wood on the front line, scrawling a letter on Boxing Day 1914:

"I am writing from the trenches. It is 11 o'clock in the morning. Beside me is a coke fire, opposite me a 'dug-out' (wet) with straw in it. The ground is sloppy in the actual trench, but frozen elsewhere. In my mouth is a pipe presented by the Princess Mary. In the pipe is tobacco. Of course, you say… But wait. In the pipe is German tobacco. Haha, you say, from a prisoner or found in a captured trench.Oh dear, no! From a German soldier. Yes a live German soldier from his own trench. Yesterday the British & Germans met & shook hands in the Ground between the trenches, & exchanged souvenirs, & shook hands. Yes, all day Xmas day, & as I write. Marvellous, isn't it?"

The letter reveals something of the dreamlike element in the events which have become known as the Christmas Truce, the peculiar, inspiring and uncategorisable events when both sides came out of the trenches and met in No Man's Land to celebrate Christmas 1914. Williamson's letter continued with a bit of background:

"On Xmas eve both armies sang carols and cheered & there was very little firing. The Germans (in some places 80 yds away) called to our men to come and fetch a cigar & our men told them to come to us. This went on for some time, neither fully trusting the other, until, after much promising to 'play the game' a bold Tommy crept out & stood between the trenches, & immediately a Saxon came to meet him. They shook hands & laughed & then 16 Germans came out. Thus the ice was broken. Our men are speaking to them now. They are landsturmers or landwehr, I think, & Saxons & Bavarians (no Prussians). Many are gentle looking men in goatee beards & spectacles, and some are very big and arrogant looking. I have some cigarettes which I shall keep, & a cigar which I have smoked. We had a burial service in the afternoon over the dead Germans who perished in the 'last attack that was repulsed' against us. The Germans put 'For Fatherland & Freedom' on the cross. They obviously think their cause is a just one."

Williamson failed to tell his parents about the wiring party he had joined in No Man's Land on Christmas night, just as he failed to tell them the one he had been out on a few days before, when he had come under fire and hid in a green shellhole, raving with fear. On Christmas Eve, despite the moon, his wiring party had not been fired on, even though the German trenches were in a turnip field just 50 yards away, and he and his comrades were horribly visible in the moonlight. "We worked with a lightness and joy until 2am & then filed back to the water dripping blockhouses," he wrote later. "The next day the miracle was manifest."

Williamson, perhaps more than most of those taking part, saw the events as a miracle. There is an immediacy about the description in his letter home that goes beyond so many of the others, and of course so many of the accounts of the truce have been written with the advantage of years to think about it since. Nearly half a century later, Williamson fictionalised the events in his novel *A Fox Under My Cloak*, describing crawling through No Man's Land on Christmas night and hearing 'Silent Night' sung from the enemy trenches:

> "It was all so strange. It was like being in another world, to which he had come through a nightmare; a world finer than the one he had left behind, except for beautiful things like music, and springtime on his bicycle in the country."

The incident changed his life. The revelation that the other side was not just human, but regarded the struggle in similar terms to the allies, made him look on the war in a new light, informed by his growing awareness that he was himself partly German. The truce made him an idealist. The enemy soldiers he met were cold, frightened and idealistic, just as he was. The strange and moving story of the Christmas Truce, with German and British soldiers – and many other nationalities too – singing carols, swapping food, drink and tobacco, was a vision of a world where the ordinary people understood that the First World War, for all its heroism and purpose, was still the central tragedy of the European story.

Very little in history was as completely spontaneous, certainly as unexpected, as this little truce between the warring nations – happening beneath the noses of the generals, apparently without guile and, at least for the British and Germans, without political undercurrents. It is one of those very rare moments during the bloody twentieth century which provide a glimmer of light. It is, depending on your attitude, a great overlooked moment of the past century – spontaneous, hopeful and filled with possibility – or a betrayal of the cause, a lazy abdication of responsibility.

Our difficulty now is to understand those events as they originally appeared at the time. We see the trenches through the eyes of educated people a century later. We have read the war poets, heard and imbibed the phrase 'lions led by donkeys'. We regard the slaughter of the First World War not just as an avoidable catastrophe – which it clearly was – but as a pointless struggle. But that is not how those who took part in the Christmas Truce regarded it. To see the events of those few days a little more clearly, we have to understand the way they saw the war at the time, and that means putting aside what we know about what came later – from the Somme and the tanks to poison gas – and try to travel back in time to the moment when Europe first set out so hopefully to war, and first began to realise the human consequences of stalemate.

I

"I will not say a single word in disparagement of the German people. They are a great people, and have great qualities of head and hand and heart. I believe, in suite of recent events, that there is as great a store of kindliness in the German peasant as in any peasant in the world; but he has been drilled into a false idea of civilisation. It is efficient, it is capable; but it is a hard civilisation; it is a selfish civilisation; it is a material civilisation."
David Lloyd George, Queen's Hall, London, 19 September 1914

Imagine sitting in the Queen's Hall, the huge concert venue that used to be next to what is now Broadcasting House, on a warm September evening, six weeks after fighting had broken out, hearing the Welsh lilt of David Lloyd George setting out the moral justification for the war. To us now, as it did then, it sounds high-minded, humane and convincing:

"Belgium has been treated brutally. How brutally we shall not yet know. We already know too much. But what had she done? Had she sent an ultimatum to Germany? Had she challenged Germany? Was she preparing to make war on Germany? Had she inflicted any wrong upon Germany which the Kaiser was bound to redress? She was one of the most un-offending little countries in Europe. There she was — peaceable, industrious, thrifty, hard-working, giving offence to no one. And her cornfields have been trampled, her villages have been burnt, her art treasures have been destroyed, her men have been slaughtered — yes, and her women and children too. Hundreds and thousands of her people, their neat, comfortable little homes burnt to the dust, are wandering homeless in their own land. What was their crime? Their crime was that they trusted to the word of a Prussian King."

Reading Lloyd George's words today, spoken when he was Chancellor of the Exchequer and the leader of those radical Liberals who had opposed the Boer War, gives a small glimpse of the way people felt at the time, and their outrage at the violation of Belgian neutrality. It is a speech that retains its power to move. It explains a little of what seems so incoherent to people a century later, brought up with the revisionist view of the conflict or the musical *Oh, What a Lovely War!*. It explains something of why people rallied to the flag and volunteered in such numbers, and amidst such enthusiasm.

Those who took part in the Christmas truce that year, on the British side, were mostly volunteers rather than embittered conscripts. They were outraged at the invasion of Belgium and the stories of atrocities. The bayoneting of babies seems insane and hard to believe, and can easily be discounted. These kind of rumours tend to emerge in war, and there were similar stories about the marlinspike issued to British troops which the Germans believed was designed to take out the eyes of prisoners. But the basic stories about civilians, including women and children, from the occupied areas of Belgium and France, rounded up as slave labour or slaughtered in reprisals, were unfortunately all too true. The English press was vitriolic, but there was enough truth – apparent to those more thoughtful people who could see beyond the immediate headlines – to drive them in huge numbers to enlist.

Most of those who had joined at the outbreak of war did not take part in the retreat from Mons, the terrifying defence of Le Cateau, the fightback on the Marne and the month-long stalemate at the Battle of the Aisne, when the soldiers first found themselves sheltering in trenches. What followed as a result was a stalemate, a semi-permanent double line of defensive trenches stretching 450 miles from the English Channel to the Swiss border. The tiny British force defended 21 miles of this and the Belgians 15 miles. The frontline bulged around Ypres, and here there was one more concerted attempt to break out of the trenches.

The First Battle of Ypres at the end of October 1914 was the German equivalent of the disaster of the Somme for the British 18 months later. The reservists on the British side, flung into the frontline with little or no training, found themselves scything down the approaching enemy with rifle fire, over and over again.

The realities of defensive modern warfare were just beginning to dawn on both sides. This horrific new phenomenon, trench warfare, and the grim realisation that there was going to be no instant victory on either side, was the background to the strange Christmas events that followed. The British and French had rejected an offer to mediate by the American president Woodrow Wilson, and were talking now about the need for total victory to demilitarise Germany. The Germans had been first shocked, and then enraged, that the British had come into the war against them – it was said that the Kaiser had nearly fainted when he heard the news (and had to be revived with a glass of champagne). It was now becoming clear, after stalemate on the Western Front, that this was now a war of national survival for the Germans. Their new slogan was 'Peace Through Victory'.

But if the German side was at the limit of their supply lines, and found themselves unable to break through the trench defences of the allies, the enormous effort to prevent the Germans breaking through to Paris had exhausted the French and all but annihilated the old professional British army. Even so, not everyone had grasped what had happened and what it meant. One of the few was Winston Churchill, then in the British cabinet as First Lord of the Admiralty, who realised that the cavalry charges he remembered as a young man were now an archaic anachronism, and that war "in its greedy, base, opportunistic march … should turn instead to chemists in spectacles and chauffeurs pulling the levers of aeroplanes and machine guns".

Churchill's fiefdom was the navy, and he had presided over an early victory at sea on 8 December, when two British battlecruisers overwhelmed the German raiding squadron at the Battle of the Falkland Isles. But he also knew, as a military historian, that the British had never relied on an army of conscripts. They had relied on an elite force of professionals. The exhaustion of the first five months of the war had now wiped out that professional army as a coherent force.

By the end of 1914, the BEF had suffered 90 per cent casualties. Not all were dead, and many would return after recovery and rest. Some were also prisoners. But even so, they had already lost 16,200 killed, tiny compared to the other sides and with what came later, but enough to remove the core experience from the BEF. Reinforcements were on their way, but the 22 territorial battalions and six yeomanry regiments that arrived in the British sector before Christmas were not exactly in the first flush of youth. The British commander-in-chief, Sir John French, complained to the War Office on 16 December that some of them were over 50 and hadn't fired a rifle since the Boer War.

All they could do now was wait until a new citizen's army could be recruited and reinforcements from across the British Empire could arrive, and bring with them some chance of a breakthrough. The Christmas truce took place just as the new reality of this situation began to dawn. It meant exhaustion, standstill, confusion and a new kind of war where the rules were not yet understood.

II

"Lice, rats, barbed wire, fleas, shells, bombs, underground caves, corpses, blood, liquor, mice, cats, artillery, filth, bullets, mortars, fire, steel: that's what war is. It is the work of the devil."
Otto Dix, German expressionist artist

The first people to be horribly aware that this was different were the frontline professional officers. "The papers still give the impression that war is an affair of dash and class," wrote an anonymous officer from the BEF in the papers on 18 November. "This is not what is happening. The bravery of our men, and they are splendidly brave, consists of sitting, often for days and nights, in sodden trenches, with the terrifying and earth-shaking concussions of shells."

This was the new reality. War had changed, and – although the idea of trench warfare is only too familiar to us now – it was extremely unfamiliar to the people facing it for the first time. This was also precisely the time of year when trench warfare was most uncomfortable. The flat landscape where the British trenches lay were mainly in Flanders, and was at sea level, with German trenches on slightly higher ground. There was a desperate shortage of warm clothing and equipment and the different strategies of both sides dictated different kinds of trenches. The Germans just needed to stay put behind defensive buttresses; the allies had to push them back – and, as a result, their trenches were makeshift affairs, with none of the comforts and innovations that came later.

It was, of course, worse than that. The boots of the British soldiers were not standing up to constant exposure to this kind of mud and were not protecting their feet. Ironically, there was also a chronic lack of water in the field hospitals to wash wounds. Gangrene was a constant problem. Without antibiotics, many wounds simply led to fatal infections. Nor was there any water for basic cleanliness. Soldiers urinated into tin cans and flung them into No Man's Land, where they added to the possibilities of disease.

Trench living was, for those encountering it for the first time, a kind of unbelievable hell, lived out in front of a stretch of land between the two lines for which the term No Man's Land had just been coined by Major Ernest Swinton, Kitchener's official war correspondent at the front. Out there, the corpses from patrols or brief skirmishes would stay rotting for weeks, if not months, their flesh eaten away by rats; their stench wafting over to the former friends and enemies alike. The military believed that, in the circumstances, it was absolutely vital to keep soldiers busy. They wanted them out on patrol, organising sorties to straighten the line, staying offensive, yet most people on the frontlines could see that most of this activity was not just dangerous, but pointless. The more thoughtful commentators and military minds doubted whether human beings could stand it.

It was particularly hard for new arrivals to grasp the realities. Lionel Tennyson of the Rifle Brigade described watching the Seaforth Highlanders next door. "A most extraordinary lot of men," he wrote. "If a shell has not come over for twenty minutes or so, they get out of their trenches and start exposing thrmselves as if no battle was on. The consequence is that many get killed unnecessarily."

Paul Hub from Wurttemberg explained the miseries of trench life to his wife:

"My dear Maria, I feel so terrible I'd rather not write to you … every day spent here makes it clearer to me how beautiful home is – what a stirring of feelings that word 'home' brings out in me. I have lived through such horror recently, no words can describe it, the tragedy all around. Every day, the fighting gets fiercer and there is no end in sight. Our blood is flowing in torrents… all around me is gruesome devastation. Dead and wounded soldiers, dead and dying animals, horse cadavers, burnet-out-houses, churned up fields, vehicles, clothes, weapons…. I didn't think war could be like this."

The British official history noted a "considerable lethargy and a marked disinclination" to dig among the soldiers. Perhaps this was hardly surprising. It must have felt too much like digging their own graves. There were, in any case, hardly any picks or shovels, and the duck boards took a long time to arrive. The equipment did not suit the situation. Trench mortars had to be improvised and often the makeshift bombs simply landed back in front of the person firing them, and it would become increasingly clear in the weeks ahead that shells were running dangerously short.

As the rain began to fall in the final weeks of the year, and the temperature dipped, the effect was disabling. "I have never seen men in such a state of mud and so tired," wrote Brigadier-General Frederick Heyworth, watching men coming out of the trenches.

Nor was there nearly enough warm clothing for the BEF which had, after all, had embarked in high summer. The army took this seriously. When soldiers came out of the line, they would file through a washhouse, they handed their underwear over and it was replaced, while their own was washed and ironed and given to the next soldiers that came through. While they were in the bath, their uniforms were ironed to get rid of the lice.

Sir Douglas Haig, commanding I Corps, kept a diary and it is full at this stage of the war with these bathing arrangements. Like so many senior officers, he was only too aware of history. The lethal incompetence of the British authorities, so unprepared for the trenches in the Crimea, then only six decades before, overshadowed everything. Haig seems not just to have been deeply concerned about the conditions in the trenches, but concerned also to prove to posterity that he was active on the issue.

Colonel Swinton was one of the first commentators to articulate the reality of the trenches to an audience back home. His column on the subject was written on 21 December and syndicated in the British papers on Boxing Day:

"Seamed with dugouts, burrows, trenches, and excavations of every kind and fitted with craters, it is bounded on the front by a long discontinuous irregular line fringed with barbed wire and broken by saps wriggling still more to the front. This is the Ultima Thule, beyond, of width varying according to the nature of the fighting and of the ground, is neutral territory, the no-man's land between the hostile forces. It is strewn with the dead of both sides, some lying, others caught or propped on the sagging wire, where they may have been for days, still others half buried in craters or destroyed parapets. When darkness falls, with intinite caution, an occasional patrol or solitary sniper may explore this gruesome area, crawling among the debris – possibly of many fights –

over the dead bodies and inequalities of the ground till some point of vantage is gained whence the enemy's position can be examined or a good shot obtained."

This may have been the first systematic description of the truth about the front for many civilians back home. What he failed to add in this despatch, but is absolutely crucial when it comes to understanding the truce, was just how narrow No Man's Land could be. "Everything is quite, quite different and more insane than you could suppose possible," wrote Sergeant Gustav Sack, the future war poet, serving on the Somme. "You don't see anything, although the wicked enemy is only 3-400m away, but you hear plenty."

Here was the point. Each side could hear each other's coming and goings, their songs and stresses, a good deal of the time. They got used to it. Here is Second Lieutenant Denis Barnett, serving with the Prince of Wales' Leinster Regiment, writing a letter home in March the following year:

"I had a conversation with a German the other morning. It began just at dawn: 'Guten morgen, Allyman', and we soon got going. I told him about the Kaiser, and he said we were all sorts of things I didn't know."

Barnett also told a story about a colleague who had left his trench without permission to search a farm for chickens, and ran into a German soldier doing the same. Neither had a rifle, so they nodded at each other politely and moved on. It was this existing, unrequested intimacy that seems to have made the tacit agreements possible when they began to emerge, once stalemate had set in.

Early in December, a German military surgeon reported regular half hour truces with the French in the evenings, to bury the dead and exchange newspapers.

Royal Engineer Andrew Todd wrote to *The Scotsman*, explaining that the front line trenches were only 60 yards apart at one place, and the two sides had become very 'pally', even throwing newspapers across to each other. "On a quiet night, we used to sing to each other," wrote one British private, "sometimes alternate verses of the same tune... they often sang their own words to God Save the King."

God Save the King muddled the British, who often took the tune as an immense compliment by their opponents, who may actually have been singing Heil dir im Siegerkranz, the imperial anthem of the German empire, which used the same tune.

"We were close," wrote 17-year-old Private Albert Moren, of the 2nd Queen's Regiment to his parents. "We threw tins of bully beef over to them or jam or biscuits, and they threw things back. It wasn't done regular, just an occasional sort of thing." Although the German side were in some ways more comfortable in their trenches, they did like the British tins of bully beef, or corned beef, which was at that time the cornerstone of British army rations.

Some of this must have taken place away from the watchful eyes of regimental staff, but not all. They must have understood, as well as the men in the front line, that a little 'live and let live' was a humane approach – and one with advantages in bad weather or when they needed to bury the dead. But clearly not all the officers understood.

Michael Holroyd, a junior officer in the Hampshire Regiment, on the eastern edge of Ploegsteert Wood, writing on Christmas Eve, described a rumour he had heard about a regiment he described as 'the Wessex'. He said the Germans in their trench would shout "half time, Wessex!", and a young singer would stand on their parapet and sing. When an officer arrived from either side, they would all fire in the air until he had been sufficiently impressed with their 'fighting spirit'. "One excellent feature is the relations with the enemy," he wrote.

One of those features of trench life which has been largely forgotten was the humour, and not just the jokes and ragging with each other, but with the enemy too – a few yards away. They ranged from the lifesize picture of a man with his thumb at the end of his nose, which was erected above the Ypres trenches in the spring of 1915 whenever there was a German bombardment, right through to the constant calls of 'waiter!'

The waiter joke requires a little explanation, but it is key to understanding the Christmas truce. There were more than 27,000 Germans working in London alone in 1911, and there were German communities around Tottenham Court Road, as well as in the centres of a number of British cities, and huge numbers of German émigrés were working as waiters. One reason there were enough translators to manage an unofficial truce was because there were so many Germans working in the UK until the outbreak of war. But it also allowed the English endlessly to repeat the same old joke, shouting 'waiter!' across No Man's Land.

For the black humour of the battlefield, listen to Albert Vivian, a lance corporal in the 4th Middlesex Regiment at the Battle of Mons. He was just relaxing when a sentry rushed in and shouted: "Blimey! Corporal, grab your blomin' pop gun and have a dekko at the Kaiser's bodyguard prancing down the road, but be bleedin' careful."

Vivian and his friends stared at them in horror, and when the firing started, they picked up their rifles and wiped them out. There were terrible casualties and the regiment felt mainly relief when the German stretcher bearers arrived to fetch their wounded, just 30 yards away. "How would you like your eggs fried?" shouted one black humorist.

Someone on the German side shouted back: "We were inclined to season them with too much pepper."

But there is a more telling story because it reveals the familiarity that many in the German trenches shared with English humour, and it took place that December, when the Somerset Light Infantry was supporting the Rifle Brigade in a raid on the enemy trenches. They went over the top at 5.30pm, only to find the trenches empty, full of water, but with barbed wire hidden under the water.

As the Somersets approached, a voice from behind the German wire shouted: "Come on the 'Sets'!"

**

It was during this peculiar impasse in the war that the Pope intervened and proposed a Christmas truce. Pope Benedict XV was newly elected to the post in September 1914 (he had only been created a cardinal in May), and was immediately confronted with a global conflagration. His considered response came on 7 December, begging the adversaries to "cease the clang of wars while Christendom celebrates the feast of the world's redemption".

A senior staff officer, Lord Loch, articulated the official view – and it still is the view of historians who are sceptical about the significance of the truce that did happen: "War is a brutal and loathsome business and the soonest way to end it is to make war with guns whole heart and soul, regardless of cost and regardless of all the amenities of peacetime."

US senator William Kenyon made a second attempt, proposing a 20-day truce over the Christmas period. Neither side replied.

Instead, the British were turning to the new reality of trench warfare. It was not their problem alone. It was clear to their generals that no progress would be made for some time. To the north, the stolid, dependable and unimaginative Douglas Haig commanded I Corps. At the southern end was the independent-minded General Sir Horace Smith-Dorrien. There was a total of 270,000 men on the British side, including the Cavalry Corps under General Sir Edmund Allenby. Most of them were aware of the deficiencies of their chief, Sir John French, and assumed that something would shortly change.

Smith-Dorrien, who appears often in this story, was a fascinating character – one of the only survivors as a young officer of the massacre of Isandlwana in the Zulu Wars. He never got on with French and was writing daily diary entries sent to the King, which was unlikely to endear him to his commander. French had not forgiven Smith-Dorrien for failing to obey his order to retreat after the Battle of Mons. Smith-Dorrien had realised that the British were in danger of being divided and had decided to stand and fight at Le Cateau, a controversial decision. He had shocked young officers at Sandhurst at the passing out parade that year by telling them that a European war would leave civilisation in ruins. He would lose his job the following year, one of the few imaginative commanders who might have avoided the humanitarian disaster that was to come on the Western Front.

The First Battle of Ypres was over but the fighting was still going on in the middle of December. French was not impressive at his briefing to commanders on 14 December and the first of a series of mini-engagements followed, along the lines that would become so familiar – bombardments which were too short, which failed to break up the barbed wire or which disastrously landed on the attacking troops. Grenades which turned out to be inferior to the German ones. Successes not followed up. Mud that had been too deep. It was these skirmishes which had left so many dead in No Man's Land which were buried at Christmas. These sorties were also reported as a complete success. "A beautiful epitaph for those poor boys who were little better than murdered," wrote the war hero Billy Congreve.

There was also a strategic imperative behind the action. The British wanted the Germans to believe that the Battle of Ypres was still going on, so that they did not withdraw their troops and send them to threaten other parts of the line or – worse – send them to face the collapsing Russians on the Eastern Front. But for soldiers and officers in the front line, the aggressive policy of preventing boredom by what seemed to be futile and lethal activity was one of the factors that contributed in the mood that surfaced during the Christmas truce.

Some of the bitterest battles involved Indian troops, already suffering in the cold. The Meerut and Lahore divisions of the Indian Corps attacked in the Festubert region on the morning of 19 December, together with the Gurkhas. It was cold and wet and the preliminary bombardment has stopped after only four minutes and the Sikhs found themselves pinned down in muddy beetroot field by murderous fire. Despite this, about 100 Punjabi Moslems reached the opposite trench and held it all day, refusing to surrender. Only three made it back.

At dawn the next day (20 December), there was a heavy bombardment from the other side and an attack over about six miles of the British sector of the front. In the north, the Manchester and Suffolk regiments advanced to rescue the Indian Corps. In the south, the Meerut divisions held firm, standing day after day in freezing water up to the knees. By the following morning, Haig's reinforcements from I Corps had arrived, including the Cameron Highlanders, and the flurry was over. Total casualties from the Indian Corps were 2,600, from I Corps 1,400.

In the middle of this action, Sir John French crossed the Channel, now full of confidence, to meet Prime Minister H. H. Asquith at Walmer Castle on the coast. Although the full horror of what lay before them was now clear to more thoughtful members of the government and military, it was not yet clear to French. Asquith was already infuriated by some of tbe public pronouncements of the generals. His daughter Violet wrote afterwards to her friend, the poet Rupert Brooke, that French had been "amazingly optimistic about things!" French gossiped that the only Germans taken prisoner recently had been professors, and said that a sudden collapse by the Germans was quite possible. It was this kind of blind optimism that was leading both sides towards disaster.

Among those who could see things more clearly was Lloyd George, who was beginning to see how the peacetime systems of administration were failing to cope with the requirements of this kind of overwhelming conflict. They were already rationing shells and ammunition for the forces at the front, which would eventually explode as a national scandal the following year. "Had I not been a witness to the deplorable lack of provision, I should not have thought it possible that men so responsibly placed could have so little forethought," he wrote to the Prime Minister on New Year's Eve.

The two sides licked their wounds in the last days before Christmas. The night of 21/22 December was freezing cold. Sleet fell. The following night was colder still, the fragile air broken by a continuing French bombardment to the south of the British lines. The mood was as cold as the weather. Private Edward Roe of the East Lancashire Regiment described an incident he had witnessed near Neuve Chapelle:

"One brave German carried a badly wounded Somerset in on his back. He was thanked and granted a safe passage back to his own lines. Without a doubt, on the British and German sides of the barbed wire, there are educated men; men who fear God; men who try to live up to the doctrines of their religion, faith, hope and charity."

Lieutenant Geoffrey Heinekey of the 2nd Queen's Westminster Rifles was writing to his mother about the recent flurry of activity in the trenches:

"A most extraordinary thing happened … some Germans came out and held up their hands and began to take in some of their wounded, and so we ourselves immediately came out of our trenches and began bringing in our wounded also. The Germans then beckoned to us and a lot of us went over and talked to them and they helped us bury our dead. This lasted the whole morning and I talked to several of them and I must say they seemed extraordinarily fine men."

III

"During the present week a wave of cold air had been gradually sneaking over western Europe form the northward, and, in spite of a few minor fluctuations, the tendency has been for the thermometer to descend slowly to a seasonable wintry level."
The Times, 24 December 1914

The meaning of the word 'morale' was pretty fluid. What politicians and the public meant by the word was 'mood', but there was an extra dimension to it when it was used by the military, which meant 'readiness to fight'. The major threat to morale was not then just boredom or the weather; it was the very proximity of the enemy. As early as 5 December, Smith-Dorrien issued the following directive to II Corps:

> "It is during this period that the greatest danger to the morale
> of troops exists. Experience of this and of every other war
> proves undoubtedly that troops in trenches in close proximity
> to the enemy slide very easily, if permitted to do so, into a
> 'live and let live' theory of life...officers and men sink into a
> military lethargy from which it is difficult to arouse them
> when the moment for great sacrifices again arises...the
> attitude of our troops can be readily understood and to a
> certain extent commands sympathy...such an attitude is
> however most dangerous for it discourages initiative in
> commanders and destroys the offensive spirit in all ranks...
> The Corps Commander therefore directs Divisional

Commanders to impress on subordinate commanders the absolute necessity of encouraging offensive spirit... Friendly intercourse with the enemy, unofficial armistices, however tempting and amusing they may be, are absolutely prohibited."On the German side, the commanders were – if anything – even more concerned. Falkenhayn said that fraternisation must be "discouraged most energetically". But another icy wind from the North Sea began to blow a few hours before Christmas and it intensified the human sense that both sides were, in some ways, facing a common enemy in the weather.

The raw materials for exchange were also arriving at both fronts. Princess Mary's Soldiers and Sailors Christmas Fund was distributing small rectangular boxes of cigarettes, pipe tobacco and a letter from the King, saying "May God protect you and bring you home safe". Special sweet tins were arriving for non-smokers. Cadbury's were sending chocolate; puddings were arriving from the *Daily Mail.* Normal rations and ammunition were being held up for the delivery of 300,000 Christmas boxes for the front. The Belgians and French were also getting tobacco pouches and the Germans were getting pipes carrying a picture of Crown Prince Friedrich Wilhelm.

The relevance of this was that most frontline troops had nowhere to keep their Christmas presents, so they were available to be exchanged. One witness described piles of abandoned plum puddings behind the lines, the surplus presents from the *Daily Mail.*

One of the first signs that something unusual may have been happening was only a few days after the Pope's intervention, on 11

December. It had begun, so often, because both sides needed some kind of relief from the mud, and to bury their dead. But this time, near Armentières, the Germans threw over big chocolate cake into the British trench. "We propose having a concert tonight as it is our captain's birthday, and we cordially invite you to attend," said a note accompanying the cake, as reported in the *Daily Express.* "Provided you will give us your word of honour as guests and you agree to cease all hostilities between 7.30 and 8.30... When you see us light the candles and footlights at the edge of our trench at 7.30 sharp, you can safely put your heads above your trenches, and we shall do the same and begin the concert."

The British were a little more circumspect, though they applauded each song. Then a big voice came from the German side: "Please come mit us into the chorus."

"We'd rather die than sing German," shouted one of the British wags.

The Germans replied with wit: "It would kill us if you did."

Then it was the Watch on the Rhine, and it was the end of the concert. These elements were to be repeated features of the truce – gifts of food, candles on the trenches, jokes and the Watch on the Rhine.

It was a good story for the British press, but it was already clear that other incidents were relatively common. "Weird stories in from the trenches about fraternising with the Germans," wrote Smith-Dorrien in his diary. "They shout at each other and offer to exchange certain articles and give certain information in one place, by arrangement. A bottle was put out between the trenches, and then they held a competition to which could break it first."

It wasn't supposed to be like that. Late in the afternoon of December 23, at St Yvon, above PloegsteertWood, Lieutenant

Bruce Bairnsfather of the 1st Royal Warwickshire Regiment felt a "sense of strangeness" in the air. Bairnsfather was to be the great cartoonist of the war, Old Bill. "It was just the sort of day for peace to be declared," he wrote.

Already that morning, Lieutenant Malcolm Kennedy of the Cameron Highlanders, watching his men in kilts bailing mud out of the trench, peered out in astonishment to see the Germans in the open, waving their arms about to show they were unarmed. Was it some kind of trick? What should he do? He shouted to his company commander for instructions. "Don't shoot," said his captain. "But count them!"

This reply is significant. It implies no great surprise. The evidence, such as there is, suggests that the truce was not wholly unexpected by the junior and middle-ranking officers. They needed some kind of break in the self-defeating deadlock – to bury the dead, repair their trenches and just relax a little to face the terrible weather. This simple reply seems to point towards this. It wasn't seeking a truce, but when the opportunity presented itself, the regimental officers seemed to see the advantages.

But Kennedy, like so many others, were also worried that this brazen behaviour might be some kind of ruse to lull them into a false sense of security while planning a night raid. On the left of the Cameronians were soldiers of the Royal Berkshire Regiment. Later in the day, Kennedy discovered that they had done more than simply count. They had let a couple of German soldiers come all the way across No Man's Land. According to Kennedy, one of them had said that he hoped the war would end soon as he wanted to return to his former job as a taxi driver in Birmingham.

Light snow began to fall that afternoon and the temperature lifted slightly. After nightfall that evening, it was the Berkshires that saw what was to be a defining feature of the nights that were to follow. Suddenly, there were small Christmas trees on the parapets of the enemy trenches, lit with candles. It was the work, as it turned out, of Sergeant Lange of XIX Corps, made up mainly of Saxons from Leipzig (he was in the 107th Infantry Regiment). He told an Australian woman in Leipzig the following year how a few of the Berkshires crawled out of their trenches to see what was happening. The Saxon soldiers explained that nothing was more important than Christmas and they crawled back again.

Not much later that night, the Berkshires were back to say that two of their own officers were waiting just behind the barbed wire to speak to the German major. Between them, they agreed an informal truce for their area for Christmas Eve and Christmas Day.

An editorial in the *Manchester Guardian* the next morning wrote that: "It will be strange if one of those truces arranged tacitly by the men and winked at by the commanders does not occur tonight, in order that, if possible, the Germans may find something to take the place of Christmas trees and the English something to take the place of holly in the trenches..." It is more evidence that the Christmas truce was, in some ways, already under way some time before Christmas. It was predictable and predicted.

**

The next morning, Christmas Eve, dawned cold and clear, bracing and beautiful. British planes swept over the lines and were shot at by the Germans   At Lille to the south, now in German hands, the Royal Flying Corps droped a padded plum pudding on the enemy airfield (they responded the following day with a bottle of rum dropped on the British airfield to the west).

Very early, Captain Robert Hamilton of the Royal Warwickshire Regiment was marching his men back to the lines near St Yves in front of Ploegsteert Wood, to relieve the Royal Dublin Fusiliers. It was still dark. As the exhausted, muddy Dubliners trudged past, one of the officers said: "The Germans want to talk to you".

Hamilton was unsure what this was likely to mean, but he found it was the literal truth as soon as his men were in their positions. The enemy was apparently trying to communicate with them.

"Are you the Warwicks?" shouted one across No Man's Land

"Come and see," shouted one wit.

"You come half way and we'll come half way and bring you some cigars."

Nobody moved on the English side. This was less predictable. Hamilton's erstwhile batman (servant) Ginger Gregrory asked if he could go. "Yes," said Hamilton, "but at your own risk."

Gregory climbed out of the trench and made his way across the 70-yard turnip field which represented No Man's Land. Half way across, he found three German soldiers. Two were unarmed and the third was pointing a rifle at him. The rifle was lowered and he was given a cigar. They said they needed to talk to an English officer. Gregory walked back, nervously looking behind him.

In the remaining hours of darkness, the shouted negotiations continued between the trenches. "After a great deal of shouting across, I said I would meet him at dawn, unarmed," wrote Hamilton later.

By mid morning, in many sections of the British line, it was unusually quiet. "Things went positively dead," wrote one field artillery captain. "There was not a sound; even our pet sniper went off duty." But we should not exaggerate the quiet. As many as 98 British soldiers died on Christmas Eve, many of them the victims of sniper fire. A German aeroplane dropped a bomb on Dover: the first air raid in British history.

In London, the celebrations were a little muted, but the expectations were high. Those reading the newspapers that morning could read the *Times* columnist at the front. He had been asking every soldier he met – British, French and Belgian – what they were planning to do for Christmas and "I have yet to receive an unenthusiastic answer".

There were excited scenes at some of the railway stations, Victoria in particular, as troops came home on leave for Christmas, but there were no military bands to accompany them. A large party of Sikh soldiers from a hospital in the New Forest were met at Waterloo Station by the Under-Secretary of State for India, who had agreed to show them around London. And all the time, even along the south coast of England, the guns in France were still audible as faint, deep booms on the air.

In the battered city of Ypres, a group of medical students from the English Red Cross spent the morning of Christmas Eve exploring the ruins of the cathedral. To their surprise, they found the organ was still in working order. One of them sat down to play and the sound wafted out across the rubble, mingling with the noise of the artillery bombardment in the distance.

On the German side, they were taking no chances. "The actions of the enemy allow us to recognise his intentions as to also attempt an attack upon Fricourt," ran the daily orders for the

Reserve Infantry Regiment 109 at Flers on the Somme. "Therefore no Christmas celebrations can take place; rather the further extension of the position is to be worked non-stop. Hopefully we will be able to celebrate our beautiful festival next time."

In Rome, the new Pope led the College of Cardinals in prayers for world peace. In London, choir boys from the Savoy Chapel sang carols in the wards of Charing Cross Hospital for the 60 wounded still there from the Battle of Mons. In Groningen in the Netherlands, a carol service was held for British internees led by the Anglican chaplain in Rotterdam. The menu for the evening was headed: 'Interned but not interred. 'Tis better so.'

In the East End of London, the German born baker Emil Koppner was reading and re-reading the summons he had received that morning. He was registered German, but was charged with changing the name of his business to the Bridge Street Bakery. He was unsure what this meant for him and his family, one among so many foreign émigrés caught on the wrong side.

**

Once darkness had fallen on Christmas Eve, the singing began. It wasn't that singing was at all unusual in the trenches. The Scots Guards were used to hearing their opponents singing The Watch on the Rhine and Deutschland Über Ales nearly every night and, in a Christmas mood, they decided to take them on. They sang every conceivable song they could think of. Then the Germans disarmed them by singing Tipperary.

It's a Long Way to Tipperary was treated by the allies as an alternative national anthem – though it had been written only in 1912 by a London stallholder called Jack Judge, who is supposed to have written it for a bet. It is hard to imagine now what that must have felt like for the Guards. They believed they were drowning out the other side with offensive singing, when suddenly the favourite song of the British came wafting across No Man's Land. In the same way, as the Cameron Highlanders took the places of the Devon Regiment, they were accompanied by the brass band of the Saxon XIX Corps from the opposite trenches.

"Just a line from the trenches on Christmas Eve," wrote Major Arthur Bates from the London Rifle Brigade in a pencil scrawl to his wife. "A topping night with not much firing going on & both sides singing – it will be interesting to see what happens tomorrow. My orders to the company are not to start firing unless the Germans do."

Another competitive concert was going on in front of Ploegsteert Wood, where Rifleman Graham Williams of the 5th London Rifle Brigade was watching trees with lighted candles above the opposite trench. The Germans sang Stille Nacht. The London Rifles replied with The First Nowell. The Germans clapped. When the British started O Come All Ye Faithful, the German side joined in with the Latin words Adeste Fideles.

In the trenches held by the East Lancashire Regiment, the German carols were accompanied by bursts of machine gun fire in reply from the British. The singing was aggressive too. When the Germans sang a carol, the Seaforth Highlanders responded cheekily with Who Were You With Last Night? The Germans responded with Home Sweet Home and a tune that sounded like God Save the King (Heil dir im Siegerkranz again).

At his headquarters at Hinges, two miles north of Béthune, Haig was wrapping presents. His wife Doris had sent a present for everyone on his staff and his friend Leopold de Rothschild had sent 50 sets of fur-lined gloves. The general and his servant spent the evening labelling each one individually.

An unnamed officer in the Royal Field Artillery told the *Times* that, at about 11pm, "a very excited infantry officer came along and told us that all fighting was off, and the men were fraternising in between the trenches. We had seen lights flashing on the parapets earlier in the evening and there had been a great deal of noise going on, shouts from the Germans – 'you English, why don't you come out? And our bright knaves had replied with yells of 'waiter!''."

At Beaumont to the south, behind the German lines, the church was full for the midnight service. But a French bombardment that night had weakened the ancient structures and the church collapsed. Casualties were taken to Bapaume. But there were many other churches where the bells were tolling along the lines. When they stopped, in the British sector near Polygon Wood, they could hear in the distance in the French trenches a beautiful voice singing Minuit Chrétiens. It was Victor Granier of the Paris Opera. A Belgian description also heard the same carol sung by the other side, and further down the line it was said that Walter Kirchoff of the Berlin Opera had also sung to the French.

"At midnight, firing ceased as if by mutual consent," wrote Private Edward Roe of the East Lancashire Regiment. Only an hour before, a colleague known as 'Old Jim' had been shot in the head by a stray bullet. "As I stood on the firestep, gazing out into No Man's Land with the point of a spare bayonet underneath my chin in case I might doze, I prayed to God."

On the trench to his right, they were playing Home Sweet Home. In the trench to his left, it was Keep the Home Fires Burning. The religious Roe described this as a "mockery".

Michael Holroyd of the Hampshire Regiment was writing home: "I've just been out with the doctor for an after-dinner stroll towards the enemy," he wrote. "We found the men in the intermediate lines singing loudly; not a shot from our own front or from the Bavarians opposite. The moon looks down upon a slightly misty, pale blue landscape, and bending my ear to the ground I can hear a faint whisper of a German song wafted on the breeze from their trenches half a mile away. I shall be greatly surprised if they or we fire a shot tomorrow, whatever Prussian warlords may do."

**

Christmas morning was fine and frosty at first light with fog in the low-lying areas which covered much of the trenches. At 5am, a rumour went through the East Lancashire trenches that the Hampshires next door to them were out in No Man's Land, talking to the Germans.

"Impossible, whose leg are you pulling?" said Edward Roe.

"If you don't believe me, go and see for yourself."

"And there they were, sure enough," wrote Roe later. "British and German warriors in No Man's Land, talking to each other and exchanging souvenirs. There is a Christ after all."

Soon their opposite numbers were waving at them too. For the Saxons opposite them, the first task was to bury their colleagues, who had been lying dead in the mangel-wurzel field since October. "We were thankful for that at least," wrote Roe, "for when the wind blew in the direction of our trenches, it made us sick with the foetid atmosphere of decaying bodies."

It wasn't long before the officers on both sides had met in the middle and agreed the terms of an unofficial truce, and thanks to Roe, we have the terms of the truce which – with a variety of details, tacit as well as explicit – were the terms up and down the trenches in that sector:

"1. Any action taken by the Artillery of either Army did not break our truce as we had no control over Artillery.

2. If either side received an order to fire, they would fire the first three rounds high in the air so as to give the other side time to get under cover.

3. The German machine gunners had to expend a limited amount of ammunition daily. They would fire high and blow a shrill warning blast on a whistle before firing. This waste of ammunition would take place every evening, if possible, between the hours of 5.00 pm and 6.00 pm.

4. Neither side were allowed to erect barbed wire entanglements in front of their trenches.

5. If either side fired a shot with intent to kill, the truce was declared off."

This is interesting, because it is more evidence that these local truces were more than just spontaneous events. Something similar appears to have happened in places right down the line, and even in Galicia, facing the Russians, Austrian soldiers were ordered not to fire unless provoked. Even outside besieged Przemyśl in the same region, the Russians put three Christmas trees in No Man's Land, with a note attached reading: "We wish you, the heroes of Przemyśl, a Merry Christmas, and hope that we can come to a peaceful agreement as soon as possible."

Oblivious to what was happening, General Smith-Dorrien was preparing to go to a Christmas communion service at 8am. His commander, Sir John French was motoring to Cassel to tell Marshal Foch about the reorganisation of the British command structure he had been planning, and to give him a case of English cigars. Half an hour into Smith-Dorrien's service, something was happening in the trenches opposite the Scots Guards west of Lille. Sir Edward Hulse was a dashing first lieutenant, who had already distinguished himself in a daring raid on the opposite trench at dead of night. Now, he peered out of his trench to see four Germans walking across. He detailed two of his own men to put down their weapons and meet them.

The distance between the trenches here was almost 400 yards, which was wider than most, and the Guards were nervous. "My fellows were not very keen, not knowing what was up, so I went out alone," wrote Hulse to his mother.

He was a professional solder and, although he could see the point of a truce, there were also ulterior motives and some limits. He wanted to see as much as he could of their trenches without letting them see his own. Half way across, there was a line of German barbed wire. He met them there, three privates and a stretcher bearer, and told them they must come no further. They told him they thought it was only right that they should come and wish their opposite numbers a happy Christmas.

One of the four had lived in Suffolk before the war, and had left a motorbike and a girlfriend behind there. He wanted to write her a postcard. Hulse got him to write it there and then and promised to post it.

It was at this point that he realised that he was dressed in an overcoat and an old stocking cap. It was clear his new friends thought he was a corporal and that he might therefore be able to be allowed to see a bit more of their trenches if he kept a sharp look-out. So half an hour later, he escorted them back to their wire, was given cigarettes and cigars and trudged back to his own lines. He went straight to regimental headquarters to report.

This is important for understanding what happened. If Hulse reported back to his regimental staff, many other officers must have done. The majors and colonels in the line clearly knew what was happening, even if they did not wholly approve. Either way, Hulse was back by 10am and could hardly believe what he was seeing. Despite his instructions, there was nobody in the British trench at all. Looking out across No Man's Land, he could hear the sound of Tipperary and Deutschland Über Alles, and he could see 150 or so British and German soldiers half way across. There were six or seven other crowds in the distance in either direction.

This time, he made sure he was in his proper uniform, with his cap and with his rank showing. The hubbub died down as he approached. A basic agreement was hammered out with the other side: they would not fire unless fired upon and would only go half way across the lines. The exchanges around him were particularly amusing to listen to. One Guards officer offered a German soldier a cigarette.

"Virginian?" he asked, before refusing it and explaining that he only smoked Turkish, which were at the time very much more expensive. "It gave us all a good laugh," said Hulse.

A German NCO with an Iron Cross started singing. When he had finished, Hulse suggested his own men sing Bonnie Scotland. The Germans responded and the British came back with Good King Wenceslas. Everyone then joined in Auld Lang Syne. "It was absolutely astounding and, if I had seen it on a cinematograph film, I should have sworn that it was faked," wrote Hulse later.

The soldiers they met were from the 15th Westphalians, and there is an alternative description of how the truce with the Scots Guards came about, presumably while Hulse was at regimental headquarters. A German officer called Major Thomas later described how their attention had been attracted by the British waving a white flag (in the Somme, soldiers of the German Reserve Infantry Regiment 109 had been greeted by white sheets waved by the French to set up a truce to bury their dead). Even in their descriptions long afterwards, both sides seem to have been at pains to explain that the truce was instigated by the other side.

Thomas asked for advice. Major von Blomberg said there was no time to ask for instructions. They would call a local armistice until 1pm to bury the dead. Both sides helped each other by bringing bodies to the half-way line. Thomas handed Hulse a VC and letters which belonged to an English captain who fell into their trench during attack on December 18. On an impulse, Hulse took off his silk scarf and gave it in return.

One of the Germans Hulse spoke to said he was longing to get back to London. Hulse assured him that he was too. He replied that he was sick of the war. Hulse told him that "he and any any of his friends were welcome to come over, be fed and sent on a free passage to the Isle of Man" – the main British centre for Prisoners of War at this stage of the war.

Hulse's captain, George Painter, was meanwhile still discussing the news at regimental headquarters and was left in no doubt by a visiting brigadier what his attitude should be. "George," he said. "You are not to fraternise with the Huns." But as soon as the brigadier had been seen off, Painter turned to his lieutenant and said: "Come on, Alan, show me the Huns."

Painter arrived in No Man's Land around 11.30am, as astonished as everyone else. "Well, my lads, a merry Christmas to you!" he said. "This is damned comic, isn't it!" He then produced a bottle of expensive rum from his pocket.

In the next door patch, his colleague Captain Giles Loder walked half a mile to negotiate fetching the bodies of dead Scots guardsmen in No Man's Land. He also agreed that the Germans would bring the bodies to the half way line. They brought 29 bodies for burial. Loder took their papers but was not allowed to take their rifles, which the Germans said were the spoils of war.

One German officer kept pointing to the bodies, saying in French: "Les braves, c'est bien dommage." When Painter heard about this, he walked over and gave the officer his scarf. Later that evening, a German orderly brought a pair of woolly gloves in return.

Despite his delight, Painter was as careful as Hulse in the relations with the enemy. He recalled some of his men from the fun in No Man's Land and got them to show their heads in different places above the parapet of their own trench. If anyone was watching, and they undoubtedly were, he wanted to make sure he they took the simple precaution of giving the impression that there were more of them than there actually were.

**

In a nearby section of the trenches, the chaplain of the 6th Gordon Highlanders, Esslemont Adams, was walking with Colonel Charles McLean along the lines. Together, they heard that a German patrol had encountered a British scout early that morning and asked him back for a drink, then sent him back to his own side to offer a truce. Another German party had been over to exchange souvenirs, and now the men were coming out of the trenches and surging into No Man's Land. McLean urged them back but they took no notice.

Adams saw his own duty differently. He walked towards the ditch which marked the half-way line with his arms in the air, hoping to negotiate a burial service. "I want to speak to your commanding officer," he shouted in German. "Does anyone speak English?"

"Yes," someone shouted back. "Come over the ditch." He came forward and saluted and, as he did so, a rabbit rushed out. Suddenly, everyone was dashing after it, the Gordons with their kilts flying. "It was like a football match," he wrote in the *Daily Mail* a few days later. The Germans caught it, and Adams agreed to a joint funeral service which opened with Psalm 23 – "though I walk through the valley of the shadow of death, I will fear no evil" – and a joint prayer.

After the service, a German colonel took out his cigar case and offered him one. It was an awkward moment for Adams, who was a Presbyterian and didn't approve of smoking.

"May I be allowed not to smoke but to keep this as a souvenir of Christmas here and of meeting you on Christmas Day?" he asked.

"Oh yes," said the German, with a laugh. "But can you give me a souvenir?"

Adams took off his cap, dug into the lining to find the copy of the Soldier's Prayer he always carried ("Oh God, wash me from all my sins in my Saviour's Blood, and I shall be whiter than snow").

The colonel put it in his own hat. "I value this because I believe what it says," he said. "And when the war is over, I shall take it out and give it as a keepsake to my youngest child."

**

Christmas morning was now thoroughly under way. In London, 26 swimmers had battled through the misty Serpentine that morning for J. M. Barrie's Peter Pan Cup, before a large crowd in Hyde Park. In Durham, Dean Hensley Henson was preaching about what he called the 'paradox of Christianity' – the pointlessness of singing Christmas carols "to the accompaniment of the cannon", and yet the hope that the "vigour and volume of protest" that naked aggression had aroused among the nations.

"Unfortunately, it had been found impractical to arrange a Christmas truce," said the Rev Henry Woods from the pulpit of the Temple Church in London that morning. "But they could at least hope that there was a lull in the trenches, so that the men might have an opportunity for a quiet moment with their God."

The British Royal Family was staying at York Cottage on the Sandingham Estate in Norfolk, getting ready for the traditional Christmas ceremony when they gave beef to their tenants. Asquith and his family were still at Walmer Castle on the Kent coast. The conversation around the dinner table was mainly about the imminent defeat of Russia. Only four days before, the British Military attaché in Moscow had sent a confidential memo which Lord Kitchener had circulated and it made hair-raising reading: generals with no previous experience in charge of armies, useless rifles, a chronic ammunition shortage (Russian expenditure of shells: 45,000 a day; output of Russian factories 35,000 a month).

In the German resort town of Spa, the Kaiser and his son Prince Eitel were being escorted to church by two regiments of Guards Artillery, and then onto the Grand Hotel Britannique, where 960 people were entertained to dinner with a small Christmas tree on each table. "We are attacked; we defend ourselves" said the Kaiser. "God grant that, out of the hard struggle, a rich victory may arise for us and our country."

On the Western Front, Haig and Smith-Dorrien were on their way to meet French at his headquarters at St Omer, where he was going to explain the re-organisation – the line was to be divided between the two generals. There was turtle soup and a bottle of 1820 brandy from Rothschild to accompany it.

In the Thames estuary at lunchtime, a German plane was driven off by scout planes. It was the first time and enemy plane had come anywhere near the capital.

Charles Smith of the 6th Cheshire Regiment, near Bailleul on the Messines road, described the scene at lunchtime:

> "We ate their sauerkraut and they ate our chocolate cakes, etc. We had killed a pig just behind our lines. There were quite a lot of creatures rambling about the lines, including an old sow with a litter and lots of cattle and poultry. We cooked the pig in No Man's Land, sharing it with the Boche."

Even the Indian Corps was now involved. These were the frozen Garwhals, oiled under their uniforms to keep out the cold, eating specially imported chapati flour and goats shipped in from Corsica. Opposite them were the 3rd Westphalians under Captain Walter Stennes, who had been lifting their hats on sticks to tempt the

Garwhals to shoot. Finally they crossed the line, and were soon sitting on top of the Garwhals' parapet, talking about the war.

What had begun with burying the dead, had now become a more general exchange of presents and the most enlightening conversations, especially with those in the German trenches who had been living in England.

"Wotcha, cock!" said one of the enemy to Graham Williams of the London Rifle Brigade. It turned out he had been a porter on Victoria Station.

"Are you the Warwicks?" one had shouted earlier in another set of trenches. "Any Brummagen lads here?" It turned out, in this case, that he had a wife and five children in Birmingham.

One man from the 3rd Rifle Brigade met his barber from High Holborn, and asked him to cut his hair again. He sat on an ammunition box while the process was carried out. "Maybe I should cut your throat today, yes?" said the barber, alarmingly. "Save ammunition tomorrow."

There were almost as many barbers on the other side as former waiters. "Do you know Islington?" one asked Frank Sumpter, a young private from the 1st Rifle Brigade. He did.

"Do you know the Jolly Farmer's pub in Southgate Road?" (It was still there in 2014).

"Yes, my uncle has a shoe repairing shop next door."

"That's funny, there's a barber's shop on the other side where I used to work before the war."

It was a peculiar mixture of dreamlike exhilaration and celebration. "In the afternoon, I went out and had a chat with 'our friends the enemy'," wrote Sergeant Bernard Brookes of the Queen's Westminster Rifles in the Frelinghien-Houplines sector. "Many of the Germans had costumes on which had been taken from the houses nearby, and one facetious fellow had a blouse, skirt, top hat, and umbrella, which grotesque figure caused much merriment." Near Armentières, both sides were entertained by a German juggler who had performed regularly in London.

"I honestly believe," wrote one Guards officer, "that if I called on the Saxons for fatigue parties to help with our barbed wire, they would have come over and done so."

Not everyone was happy with the truce. "This is an extraordinary state of things and I don't altogether approve of it," wrote Major John Hawksley of the Royal Field Artillery in a recently discovered letter to his sister. "Still, it gives me and my observation post a quiet time." Corporal Adolf Hitler, with the 16th Bavarian Reserve Regiment, did not approve either. In 1940, Heinrich Lugauer, a fellow dispatch runner, described him as an "embittered opponent of the fraternisation with the English ... all the talk in Christmas 1914".

Charles de Gaulle, a young lieutenant wounded in the first weeks of August, felt the same. "Trench warfare has a serious drawback: it exaggerates this feeling in everyone," he wrote. "If I leave the enemy alone, he will not bother me... it is lamentable."

There were diehard soldiers just as there were diehard officers. Michael Toudy of the Belgian grenadiers at Dixmunde wrote: "What do our top brass do here? They do nothing to stop this scandal, this first step to 'germanisation'." The British Grenadiers fired on Germans who shouted Merry Christmas and so did a section of the Seaforth Highlanders. Two soldiers from the Monmouthshire Regiment were shot on the way back from exchanging tobacco. Germans who came out of the trenches in the Aisne region were shot by their French opponents.

A more peculiar twist came when three privates from the Queen's Westminster Rifles were taken prisoner on Christmas Day, though it seems likely that they were deliberately giving themselves up (the mother of one of them committed suicide some years later, supposedly because of the shame). Captain Billy Congreve opened fire on his opposite numbers when they came out of trenches opposite the Royal Scots and Gordon Highlanders. It was, he said, "the only truce they deserve".

One sceptic, a lance-corporal in the East Lancashire Regiment, ended their particular truce on 27 December with a shot from the trenches. A German fell and three British soldiers, who had been out searching for a door to use as a roof for their dug-out were caught in the open. The lance-corporal was "very pleased with himself", according to Edward Roe, and was given a very hard time by his colleagues.

Probably the most vicious fighting was around La Boisselle on the Somme, where the French had occupied an old cemetery on the front line which the Germans called Granahof. The two sides now confronted each other exceptionally close, in trenches where they found themselves standing on buried coffin lids of the long dead. The French had dug so close that they were now less than three metres away in one place. There had been a French bombardment there at 12 noon on Christmas Eve which led to the collapse of a German dug-out. There was a concerted German attempt to re-take the cemetery at dawn on 27 December and repeated attempts over the next few days. There was certainly no truce there.

The war carried on elsewhere as well. German gunners shelled the headquarters of the Belgian army in Furnes. British seaplanes attacked Cuxhaven, the German supply port for U-boats, losing one pilot. The Norwegian steamer *Eli* was mined and sunk in the North Sea, on its way taking coal to Rouen, its crew of 15 taken off by a passing ferry and into Scarborough. Smith-Dorrien noted in his desk diary for Christmas Day that there had been "casualties: 8 other ranks" in his sector that day.

There were also a series of barely believable stories where the truce held, especially about fights. In the trenches of the Argyll and Sutherland Highlanders there was supposed to have been a boxing match followed by what would have been a duel with pistols, vetoed because it did not seem to be in the spirit of the truce. Nor is it clear what to make of the story about the single combat with bayonets, between two representatives of the two sides – one of which was supposed to have been a Gordon Highlander – in which the German was killed.

Another story, told by the Wray brothers, Frank and Maurice of the 5th London Rifle Brigade, involved a shout from the German trenches at the end of the day that the soldier needed to speak to Frank, followed by a note which read: "Yesterday, I gave my hat for bully beef ... I have grand inspection tomorrow … you lend me and I bring it back to you." The helmet was returned along with some schnapps.

One of the strangest stories was the one told of a junior officer called Harry who happened to mention, in a relaxed moment: "What I wouldn't give for a bottle of Boy now!" Boy was a nickname for a kind of champagne popularised by Edward VII.

"My dear chap, nothing easier," said the Bavarian officer he was taking to. "Decent cellar at headquarters. Come and have a noggin in our mess, won't you? Of course, it's well behind our line, but I can promise you you'll be safe. You know, we 'play the game', as you English say."

He went along and, as they went, he realised he was being taken to a farmhouse that he had reported to his superiors as having been destroyed. Inside, they opened a bottle of Veuve Cliquot 1909 and raised glasses.

"Look here, you've put me in a damned awkward position by this," said Harry. "You see, I was the observing officer when we strafed you, and I reported that the whole place had been blown to bits."

His host put down his glass. "You're a nation of sportsman," he said, "and I am as certain as I am of anything that, when you go back, you'll have forgotten everything you saw here. Isn't that so? Now, have another glass of champagne."

As they parted again, half way between the lines, his host said this: "Oh, and by the by, on Thursday (New Year's Eve), we are relieved by the Prussians. Give 'em hell. We hate them."

IV

"Had just one of these Big Mouths gathered together ten thousand footballs, what a happy solution that would have been, without bloodshed."
Lieutenant Sir Edward Hulse, Scots Guards

Chasing the hares was an icebreaker in a number of sectors and it seems to have led in some places to the legendary football match, like the one between the 133rd Saxon Regiment and the Seaforth Highlanders by Ploegsteert Wood, using their military caps to mark the goals. "It was far from easy to play on the frozen ground," wrote Lieutenant Johannes Niemann, "but we continued, keeping rigorously to the rules, despite the fact that it only lasted an hour and that we had no referee. A great many of the passes went wide, but all the amateur footballers, although they must have been very tired, played with huge enthusiasm."

The football match between the lines is one of the iconic moments of the Christmas truce, but in fact there were many football matches. And if the Germans seem to have taken the lead in most, though not all, cases of the original truce, it was clearly the British who led the way when it came to football. When the Welsh Fusiliers wanted to play, their regimental doctor walked by himself across the lines to propose a match.

The main problem was getting hold of anything remotely resembling a ball. The Lancashire Fusiliers just north of Le Touquet used an old sandbag, though it is hard to see how this could have given them much satisfaction. The French 104th and

106th Infantry Regiments reported, in rather shocked tones, that the Argyll and Sutherland Highlanders had bought a football from the Germans in return for a bottle of rum.

It was the Seaforths who fascinated the other side because they were wearing kilts. "At this soccer match, our privates soon discovered that the Scots wore no underpants under their kilts so that their behinds became clearly visible any time their skirts moved in the wind," said Niemann, interviewed in Hamburg in 1969. "We had a lot of fun with that and, in the beginning, we just couldn't believe it."

It was also the Argylls who suggested that the ball problem should be solved by sending a cyclist behind their lines to find one, while they cooked a huge stew of bully beef, around large fires in No Man's Land.

The London Rifles also used a real ball. "Even as I write (dusk)," wrote Sergeant Bob Lobell, "I can scarcely credit what I have seen and done. It has been a wonderful day."

Even a real ball, in those days of leather and stitching, was hard pressed to hold up to the conditions of mud, ice and damp. This is Private Ernie Williams of the Cheshire Regiment:

"A ball appeared from somewhere, I don't know where, but it came from their side ... They made up some goals and one fellow went in goal and then it was just a general kickabout. I should think there were a couple of hundred taking part. I had a go at the ball. I was pretty good then, at 19, everybody seemed to be enjoying themselves. There was no sort of ill-will between us ... There was no referee, no score, no tally at all."

Here again, the ball got very soggy. This was Staff Sergeant Clement Barker from the Grenadier Guards, in a letter discovered only in 2012:

> "A German looked over the trench - no shots - our men did the same, and then a few of our men went out and brought the dead in (69) and buried them and the next thing happened a football kicked out of our trenches and Germans and English played football. Night came and still no shots. Boxing day the same, and has remained so up to now..."

It appeared to be a ritual, the next stage in the truce wherever relations had progressed that far, at least where the Germans met the British. In the Warwickshire Regiment above Ploegsteert Wood, the cartoonist Bruce Bairnsfather explained on Canadian television in 1958 that someone had just produced a deflated football and inflated it.

Lieutenant Zehmisch of the Saxons, on other side to the Warwicks, wrote:

> "A couple of English brought a football out of their trench and a vigorous football match began. This was all so marvellous and strange. The English officers thought so too ... Toward evening, the officers asked whether a big football match could be held the following day, between the two positions.

Zehmisch said he could not agree definitely because they were due to be relieved the following day.

Inevitably, the talk with the Germans who had been working in the UK often came back to football. Lieutenant Hugh Barrington-Brown of the Leicestershire Regiment found himself talking to a Saxon soldier who had been a waiter in a restaurant in the Fulham Road in London, and wanted to know how Fulham was getting along in the FA Cup. Lance Corporal Hines from the Queen's Westminster Rifles reported in the *Chester Chronicle* a few weeks later that his opposite number had lived in Alexander Road in Hornsey, and he had really wanted to see Woolwich Arsenal play Tottenham the following afternoon.

The *Times* reported on a match which the London Rifles had played in front of their trench, though the official history of the regiment explicitly denies this. This may have been the same game that the Queen's Westminsters played for the Germans to watch – the other side refused to take part because "either they considered the ground too hard, as it had been freezing all night, and was a ploughed field, or their officers put the bar up".

Frank and Maurice Wray, from the London Rifle Brigade, definitely played a match because one of their team met a fellow team member on the opposite side from his own football team in Liverpool.

Back home, the British football season was in full throttle, even on Christmas Day. Aston Villa beat Blackburn Rovers 2-1, Sunderland beat Newcastle United 5-1, Liverpool beat Bolton Wanderers 1-0. Chelsea and Manchester City drew nil nil. The match between Southend United and Croydon Common in Southend was called off because of the dense fog (it was replayed at Selhurst Park on Boxing Day and they drew 1-1).

The famous football matches took place in the days that followed as well. Of course, it was the football that really scared the generals. Everyone knows what a peacemaker a game of football can be. During the General Strike in 1926, twelve years later, the historians credit the games of football between the pickets and the police as a sign that there never could have been a revolution. Perhaps that was why one unconfirmed story suggests that the East Kent (the Buffs) Regiment's football match was stopped by a furious colonel who threatened the match with machine guns.

The future poet Robert Graves joined the Royal Welch Fusiliers too late to take part in the truce, but he heard stories which he remembered imaginatively in a story published in 1962:

"No Man's Land had seemed ten miles across when were crawling out on a night patrol; but now we found it no wider than the width of two football pitches. We provided the football, and set up stretchers as goal posts; and the Rev. Jolly, our padre, acted as ref. They beat us 3-2."

And here Graves touches on one common element in the story. The Germans won 3-2, and it is extraordinary how many of these informal matches appear to have ended with that score. It is as if the extraordinary experience of playing the game drove out all memories of the actual result, and all those took part borrowed the same score – which became the only score than anyone could remember when it came to telling the story again.

The Lancashire Fusiliers near Le Touquet ended with a score of 3-2 to the other side. That was also the score of the match between the RAMC and the Saxons. A later game on New Year's Day, organised by a major in the Medical Corps, which ended with the Saxon soldiers playing God Save the King again, also ended 3-

2 to the Germans. So did the Seaforth Highlanders game against the Saxons outside Ploegsteert Wood.

One exception was the match near Ypres between the Argyll and Sutherland Highlanders and the Prussians and Hanovers, which the Argylls claimed to have won 4-1. But another report, or possibly a different match, saw the Argylls' match ending in a draw.

The football matches were a step too far for those who were most sceptical about the warm fellow feelings. Lieutenant C. E. M. Richards of the East Lancashire Regiment was already frustrated by the truce, which seemed to him to be a monumental irrelevance, and was staggered to find himself ordered by his battalion headquarters to make a football pitch in No Man's Land on Christmas night, and to challenge the enemy to a match. He didn't.

Nor was he the only one. Lieutenant-Colonel Gustav Riebensahm of the 2nd Westphalians had welcomed truce. But by Boxing Day, he was writing in his diary:

"The English are said to have told the 53rd Regiment that are exceedingly thankful for the truce because they simply had to play football again. The whole business is becoming ridiculous and must come to an end. I arranged wth the 55th Regiment that the truce will end this evening."

V

"The soldier's heart rarely has any hatred in it. He goes out to fight because that is his job. What came before – the causes of the war and why and wherefore – bother him little. He fights for his country and against his country's enemies. Collectively, they are to be condemned and blown to pieces. Individually, he knows they are not bad sorts... The lull is finished. The absurdity and tragedy renew themselves."

Daily Mirror editorial, 2 January 1915

Josef Wenzel, a regimental orderly in the same unit as Adolf Hitler near Messines, was writing a letter home: "At 3 o'clock on the morning of 26 December, we were moving forward in the trenches. Everything was frozen hard. [I] prepared myself to be met by heavy fire. But imagine my astonishment when not a shot came. The men we relieved told us that they had been exchanging things with the English, which seemed crazy to us. As proof, I found a few English cigarettes in my dugout, which tasted very good…."

Wenzel explained that, shortly after dawn, the Englishmen appeared and waved and soon the same ritual was being repeated as it had done the previous day. The Bavarians and English, who had – as he put it been "until now the fiercest of enemies shook hands, spoke to one another and exchanged things ... I will never forget this sight for the rest of my life."

Wenzel's colleagues also looked at how the British trenches were laid out, just as Hulse had peered at the German trenches the day before. The British soldiers seemed young to them, and both sides seemed impressed by the abundance of food enjoyed by the other. Like their colleagues, the Bavarians very much enjoyed the British bully beef. They enjoyed hearing about their irritation with the French. Their virtual truce lasted until 29 December, and each side kept to themselves, except during the storm on 28 December when the British came out of thir trenches to carry out repairs.

But Boxing Day was the day that news of the unofficial truces began to filter through to the top brass. Boxing Day saw General Haig concerned with other things, saying goodbye to his staff and handing over command of I Corps, then – while his staff began the search for a new headquarters to requisition – riding over to Festubert to discuss the design of grenades with generals Butler and Haking.

His colleague General Smith-Dorrien was more aware of what was going on. He sat down and wrote this confidential memo:

> "On my return I was shown a report from one section of how, on Christmas Day, a friendly gathering has taken place on neutral ground between the two lines, recounting that many officers had taken part in it. This is not only illustrative of the apathetic state we are gradually sinking into, apart also from illustrating that any orders I issue on the subject are useless, for I have issued the strictest orders that on no account is intercourse to be allowed between the opposing troops. To finish this war quickly, we must keep up the fighting spirit and do all we can to discourage friendly intercourse. I am calling for particulars as to names of officers and units who took part this Christmas gathering, with a view to disciplinary action."

It may not have been entirely coincidental that an allied bombardment was ordered of the German trenches at 9am on the morning of Boxing Day.

It was an awkward moment. Those who had taken part in the meetings in the previous days knew that the fighting would begin again sooner rather than later. Any British bombardment was bound to be extremely limited because of the rationing of shells but, even in the unaffected areas, the renewal of hostilities began to loom large. Lieutenant Vyvyan Pope of the North Staffordshire Regiment in the Frelinghien-Houplines sector was told that the German colonel had given orders to end the truce at midday, and could they keep their heads down? "I thought it was very decent of him and told him so," said Pope. In the end, there was no shooting. But, in the evening, a chocolate box was thrown into the Staffordshire's trench with the message: "We shoot to the air".

Second Lieutenant J. D. Wyatt of the 2nd Yorkshire Regiment (the Green Howards) wrote in his diary for 30 December: "A message came down the line to say that the Germans [expected] that their general was coming along in the afternoon, so we had better keep down, as they might have to do a little shooting to make things look right!!! And this is war!!"

It was from then on that local truces, organised with the agreement and certainly the knowledge of the regimental staff, began to look like something slightly different – almost a shared connivance by ordinary soldiers on both sides to avoid fighting. It was the very thing the generals feared, as well they might. It seems unlikely that anyone on either side was actively pursuing an early end to the conflict – there is certainly no evidence of that – but they may have been seeking to put off the evil day, while their officers continued to turn a blind eye because it gave them some security in which to rebuild and repair.

Hulse and the Scots Guards had spent a nervous night after their original meeting in No Man's Land because a German deserter came over to them in the night and told them to expect an attack. Nothing of the kind happened and Hulse described the confidence of most of the German soldiers he talked to – full of the imminent collapse of Russia and France. The whole business of the past three days has been extraordinary and not easy to explain," he wrote to his mother. "Yesterday (27th), shooting began again, down in the 8th Division, but although we explained to the enemy that the truce was at an end, never a shot was fired." Hulse was killed the following year.

**

The civilised world was beginning to wake up after Christmas. Boxing Day in London was a day of rain, sleet and icy wind. Madame Tussauds, the waxworks museum, opened their new exhibition of generals and admirals from the frontline – there was French and Jellicoe, Haig and Beatty. The theatres opened again. *Peter Pan* was in its eleventh year at the Duke of York Theatre. *Cinderella* was packing them in at the Aldwych, *Charley's Aunt* at the Prince of Wales Theatre and the veteran actor-manager Sir Herbert Tree was in *David Copperfield* at His Majesty's Theatre.

This was also a khaki Christmas in London, aware of the wounded filling the hospitals, the fleet at their lonely Scottish anchorage and the front just across the English Channel. That same afternoon, the German Zeppelin force was preparing for its air raid on Nancy the following day. It was a test run for the bombing of London the following year.

Yet the truce continued, certainly not everywhere, but in some sectors. Part of this was the result of the storm and "torrents of rain" that fell on 28 December and hampered Smith-Dorrien's planned inspection the following day. Haig was still scouring the countryside for an adequate chateau for his headquarters and worrying about his new staff and liaison officers. He wrote in his diary:

> "D. Braine is a stockbroker, I believe, but is very pleasant to deal with and quite quick. M. Lazare (a financier of standing, with a splendid car) will also remain with me in the capacity of 'interpreter', but his real role is to go to Paris or elsewhere to buy the necessary food and drink to supplement the rations for the whole of the Army staff."

It was during this period that Bruce Bairnsfather managed to get out and explore the ruins of St Yves village. It is his adventures, one assumes, that fed into Henry Williamson's fictionalised account where he borrows a bicycle and finds himself some way behind enemy lines.

The Warwicks were relieved in their trenches by the Dublin Fusiliers on 28 December, but the truce carried on. When the news came of a bombardment on a farm still standing in the German support lines, the frontlines knew that the German officers would be having coffee there at the time. Colonel Arthur Loveband, commanding officer of the Dublin Fusiliers, chivalrously sent a soldier over to warn them.

When the Warwicks arrived back in the trenches four days later, it was immediately clear that the informal truce still held. A dog arrived across the No Man's Land from the Germans to welcome their arrival. "How are you nicey Englishman?" said a message round its neck. "We are all well, please send the dog back". The Warwicks gave it some meat and sent it home.

By this stage, the fraternisation in No Man's Land had finished, but a long period of Live and Let Live had taken root in many sectors. The Wray brothers in the London Rifle Brigade described a drunken German found in their barbed wire on New Year's Eve who was sent to brigade headquarters as a prisoner. They sent him back with a message to say they wanted the truce to carry on until the work on the trench parapets had been finished. The Gordon Highlanders had agreed a truce that specified that there should be no shooting until January 3, though this was broken when a visiting brigadier ordered that a visible German suddenly visible in his own trench should be shot at. The shot missed.

On January 4, Robert Hamilton of the Royal Warwickshire Regiment wrote:

> "Quite pleasant and quiet all day. The dugouts are
> progressing, thank goodness. I sat on the parapet and played
> the Austrian national anthem. Four shots were fired at me, so
> I played Rule Britannia. I wonder why they didn't like the
> Austrian air."

It was difficult to go back to war. The 1st Hampshire Regiment got a message from the Saxons opposite, which said: "Gentlemen, our automatic fire has been ordered from the colonel to begin again at midnight; we take honour to award you of his fact." In the 107th Infantry Regiment on the Armentieres-Lille railway, furious officers ordered their men to fire, but they did so reluctantly. "We spent that day and the next wasting ammunition in trying to shoot stars down from the sky," Sergeant Lange told an Australian friend in Leipzig the following year. He said he had never heard such language as the officers "stormed up and down, and got, as the only result, the answer: 'We can't — they are good fellows, and we can't.' Finally, the officers turned on the men, 'Fire, or we do — and not at the enemy'."

But these were now exceptions. Historians have argued ever since about the significance of the events of Christmas 1914, ranging from those who believe it was an irrelevance to those for whom it was a moment of enormous significance – and part of that argument is the question of whether or not the truce stayed in effect in fact, if not in theory, for some weeks after Christmas. It clearly did in some parts of the British line, but whether that was because of the attitude of those who had taken part or because of the next major issue on the western Front – the serious shortage of ammunition – is not clear.

The Scots Guards, who had taken to joint singing so enthusiastically on Christmas Day were back in action on New Year's Day, trying to retake a captured trench near Givenchy. The first attack failed, and over 700 Scots Guards were sent in to take it and were thrown back with heavy losses. Once again, the casualty lists began to mount.

There is little evidence that those taking part in the truce believed this was somehow an alternative to war. They clearly never felt the need to reassure their families back home about their motives, as they described the events. Nor did the newspaper reports that followed over the next month or so, based usually on letters home passed on by their families. Nobody assumed that the fact that the war had stopped temporarily meant that the war might stop for good.

It seems likely that officers up to the rank of colonel had smiled on the events over Christmas. An anonymous infantry colonel had a letter published in the *Daily Telegraph* on 2 January, describing how he went up to the trenches on Christmas Day. As he left, he said: "there was a sudden hurrah and rush, and our men and the Germans both started running to one another, and met half-way and shook hands."

The colonel ordered his men back, but "was told they wanted a truce for the day to bury their dead, so I agreed to that." He left look-outs in the trenches just in case and went and joined the crowd. One of the Saxon soldiers acted as his interpreter and soon the colonel had agreed that "if they would have an armistice on New Year's Day, we would play them at football between our lines."

This is significant. The colonel saw nothing wrong, though he took sensible precautions, and the "sudden hurrah and rush" seems significant too – the ordinary soldiers understanding the intimacy which had grown up between both sides, but it seems to have taken them all by surprise. They *rushed* towards each other. It was humanitarian, even inspiring, but not an antidote to war.

The German press did not see it the same way. "War is no sport," wrote the *Berlin Tägliche Rundschau,* "and we are sorry to say that those who made these overtures or took part in them did not clearly understand the gravity of the situation."

The German military authorities went even further. They called it 'high treason'.

VI

*"What would happen I wonder if the armies suddenly &
simultaneously went on strike and said some other method must be
found of settling their dispute!"*
**Winston Churchill, writing to his wife after the birth of his daughter Sarah, December
1914**

Sir John French was to be relieved of his command nearly a year
later. His autobiography quotes his own diary for the post-
Christmas period, about the truce:

> "When this was reported to me, I issued immediate orders to
> prevent any recurrence of such conduct, and called the local
> commanders to strict account, which resulted in a great deal
> of trouble. I have since often thought deeply over the
> principle involved in the manifestation of such sentiments
> between hostile armies inthe field. I am not sure that had the
> question of the agreement upon an armistice on the day been
> submitted to me I should have dissented from it. I have
> always attached the utmost importance to the maintenance of
> that chivalry in war which has almost invariably characterised
> every campaign of modern times in which this country has
> been engaged. The Germans glaringly and wantonly set all
> such sentiments at defiance by their ruthless conduct of the
> present war, even from its very commencement."

There are two things worth noting here. The first is that, like many of the Western Front commanders, French seems to have re-written his diary with the benefit of hindsight. When people talk about having 'thought deeply' about an issue, what they often mean is 'thought often'. This was clearly not the way he saw things at the time. The second is that French was not alone in his feelings about 'ruthless conduct'. Other accounts of the Christmas truce written a few years afterwards add that the fraternisation had taken place before the sinking of the *Lusitania* and the introduction of mustard gas at the Second Battle of Ypres, both a few months later, and there is no doubt that this embittered the conduct of the war.

But there is a third point. When French explains that his decision "caused a great deal of trouble", there are almost no remaining records which provide clues about this. If the authorities tried to discipline the ringleaders, then the whole business was very quietly dropped. But what evidence there is suggests that, for very good practical reasons – and for reasons of humanity to their own men – the regimental commanders were in favour of local truces to bury the dead, to repair trenches and to survive the bitter weather. They may not have expected mass singing and football matches, but they turned a blind eye to the fraternisation that happened as a result. It must have been clear very quickly to the headquarters staff that there was no way they could launch a series of courts martial against regimental commanders.

The very little evidence for this can be found in the regimental history of the Norfolk Regiment. "The matter was eventually dropped and no harm was, in fact, done," it said, "seeing that our men managed to have a good look at the German defences, and took good care that the fraternisation did not spread over to their own trenches."

The consequences on the German side are equally difficult to discover now, though immediately after Christmas the German orders were more direct and threatening. "Commander Second Army directs that informal understandings with enemy are to cease. Officers ... allowing them are to be brought before a court martial."

On 28 December, Haig told Sir Henry Rawlinson, in command of IV Corps, that "no offensive on a large scale should be contemplated by GHQ at present, but it is desirable that his defence should be an active one." He underlined last phrase, and this was the core of the matter for the allied commanders. Haig never mentioned the truce in his diary, but this passage implies he was aware of it. Active defence was both an explanation for the truce – the exhaustion of the frontline troops in the face of demands for constant, apparently pointless raids and patrols – as well as an antidote. To tackle what they saw as the breakdown of morale, the military solution was more of the same.

**

A year on, after the horrors of 1915, the atmosphere was different. Seventeen months of war had sapped the humanitarian spirit and things had happened in the conduct of the war which was difficult to forgive.

Even so, there was an expectation that something would happen at Christmas the following year. The war correspondent Philip Gibbs reported that, on Christmas Day 1915, a German unit put a sign up above their trench which said 'THE ENGLISH ARE

FOOLS'. Not unnaturally, it was shot down. The next sign said 'THE FRENCH ARE FOOLS'. That was also shot down and was replaced by a third sign: 'WE ARE ALL FOOLS, LET'S GO HOME'.

There were certainly local truces in 1915, but not on the same scale as the previous Christmas. One local truce was scuppered by a furious brigadier. Two British officers were court martialled afterwards from the Scots Guards. One was cleared and the other case was quashed by the Commander-in-Chief, partly because the accused was known to be an excellent officer and partly perhaps because he was related to the Prime Minister.

During the disastrous first few days of the Somme offensive the follow year, a divisional commander refused permission to ask for a truce to fetch the countless wounded from No Man's Land, but it went ahead anyway.

In fact, chivalrous truces were – as Sir John French recognised – part of the tradition of the British army. There was a famous truce with the French during the Battle of Talavera, in the intense heat, when both sides stopped fighting and went and drew water from a stream. Also during the Napoleonic Wars, at Belle Isle off the French coast, the besieged French garrison commander asked for a truce so that the British officers could come and make a success of the ball he was holding ashore. The truce went ahead and so did the ball. There was a famous truce in mid-Atlantic in 1942, when the submarine U-156 found itself towing lifeboats full of children from the sunken liner *Laconia*.

It was obvious why regiments in the line might be open for some kind of informal truce, just as it was obvious why senior staff might have worried about this kind of arrangement – either because truces might actually be a cover for intelligence-gathering or for some kind of planned assault or because they might sap the will to fight.

It is pretty clear that few of those taking part in the Christmas Truce in 1914 believed that it might become a permanent state of affairs, however they might wish it to be. There were no political overtones as there were with truces on other fronts later in the war, especially after the Russian Revolutions in 1917. There were French truces after October 1917 which involved singing the Internationale. There was no parallel with the French Chanson de Craonne, the furious denunciation of war, which began in the French trenches in 1914 and emerged after the Verdun mutiny in 1917 ("Good-bye to life, good-bye to love, good-bye to all the women./It's all over now, we've had it for good with this awful war." – the song was banned in France until 1974).

There were certainly desperate elements to some of the other truces, with reports of soldiers breaking rifles and escaping to the other side. In one French incident in 1915, an officer told a soldier he would be shot, and he leapt out of the trench and took shelter with enemy. This was not the story of Christmas 1914, yet the spirit of 1914 was hardly peculiar to the British trenches - there are records throughout the war of French and German troops warning each other when they were about to explode a mine.

What was fascinating about Christmas 1914 was that it was spontaneous, but more than spontaneous. It seems to have been carried out with the active connivance of the officers in the front line, who deliberately hid what was going on from their senior commanders – not perhaps for humanitarian reasons, or for the sake of the enemy, but for the comfort of their own men and to bury the dead. But there is no doubt that it was also partly a response to the shared horror and fear that there might not be another, better way of winning.

**

There was also a group of influential people back home who felt the same. It isn't clear that concern about the truce seeped out of the military and into political circles. The war cabinet met for the first time after the New Year on January 5, but that was before cabinet minutes were kept so we can no longer know whether it was discussed. What we do know was that, on Boxing Day, two memos arrived on the desk of Prime Minister Asquith by two of his most intelligent strategic thinkers – Maurice Hankey of the Committee of Imperial Defence and Winston Churchill.

Even before the news of the truce had filtered back to England, they had begun to perceive the truth: that the Western Front was now bogged down in stalemate and any attempt to break it would be devastating in human lives. Why, they asked themselves, should Lord Kitchener's new volunteer armies, now under training in England, be wasted on this looming tragedy? Or, as Churchill put it, be sent "to chew barbed wire"?

On 29 December, he wrote:

"Without attempting to take a final view, my impression is that the position of both armies is not likely to undergo any decisive change – although no doubt several hundred thousand men will be spent to satisfy the military mind on the point."

Churchill and Hankey agreed: there had to be a better, more humane way to win the war. So began the ultimately ill-fated idea of forcing the Dardanelles to knock Turkey out of the war, to supply Russia and to unite central Europe on the allied side. History condemns it as wrong-headed, and with the benefit of hindsight perhaps it was, but – at the time – it united those humanitarian radicals, mainly in the Liberal Party, who could see what would happen on the Western Front and were desperate for an alternative.

On New Year's Day, still at Walmer Castle, Asquith replied asking Churchill to "put your detailed plans in hand at once".

Churchill followed it up with a memo to Asquith on the urgency of developing a tank to break the stalemate. Asquith received it on 5 January, handed it to Kitchener who passed it to the War Office technical department. They sat on it for two months and then said it was impossible. As we know, tanks were not available in any numbers until 1917.

For the rest of the month, Churchill was hammering out the basic strategy for the Dardanelles, and – as he did so – the reports of the Christmas Truce flooded the British newspapers, as relatives forwarded on the letters they had received from the front. This is how the truce influenced the push for an alternative strategy, which – thanks partly to a disastrously foot-dragging response from the generals and admirals – led to the slaughter of Gallipoli.

Violet Asquith, the Prime Minister's daughter and Churchill's friend and admirer, wrote half a century later: "Personal emotion may have burred my vision, but I saw it then and see it still as the most imaginative conception of the First World War, and one which might, had all gone well, have proved the shortest route to victory."

The ultimate tragedy of the Dardanelles, the result of poor leadership and bureaucratic inertia back home which delayed the expedition, meant that the inexorable slaughter of the Western Front had to be played out in all its horror – the great disaster of Western European history. Its failure had wider consequences: Churchill was flung from office, the Liberal Party went the same way, and arguably the Russian Revolution became inevitable. History shifted – and not because of the Christmas Truce – but for the same underlying reasons.

That is certainly how Churchill saw the years after 1914, as he wrote in his book *The World Crisis:*

"It is a tale of the torture, mutilation or extinction of millions of men, and of the sacrifice of all that was best and noblest in an entire generation. The crippled, broken world in which we dwell to-day is the inheritor of these awful events. Yet all the time there were ways open by which this slaughter could have been avoided and the period of torment curtailed."

**

There is nobody left alive who witnessed the events on the Western Front at Christmas 1914. Yet in other ways, we are not that different from those who took part. We have similar lives, live at the same addresses, visit the same theatres, use the same bus routes. We even read the same newspapers. Those of us who are old enough will have met many who lived through those years. We can understand their reactions and motivations far better than those who lived through Waterloo or Lexington.

But we see it, perhaps, too much through the perspective of what happened next: the abominable slaughter of the Somme, Verdun and Passchendaele. We can't believe our own society could endure such suffering. In fact they felt the same then, as Douglas Haig discovered shortly after these events.

Three weeks later, on 22 January, he recorded in his diary meeting the *Times* correspondent Colonel Charles Repington:

"He was anxious to know whether I thought we could ever advance on this front. He thought the German front impregnable and much doubts whether we would ever get a General Staff fearless of public opinion to incur the losses which must be suffered in any attempt to pierce the enemy's fortified front. He thought the British people would not stand heavy casualties. I replied that as soon as we were supplied with ample ammunition of high explosive, I thought we could walk through the German lines at several places."

As we know now, the British people did stand the casualties, though they may never have quite recovered.

The essence of the argument by historians since, not just about Haig but so many of the British commanders on the Western Front, was their collective failure to see what Churchill and Hankey saw over Christmas 1914: that the normal laws of war had shifted. The old days of parade ground discipline and frontal assaults had gone for good. What was so desperately needed was imagination, innovation, flair, and that was in desperately short supply. It was this background fear that the war had lost direction which accelerated the Christmas truce.

Marching through the town of Armentières after the events of the truce, British soldiers were spat at by French women in doorways for being friendly to the German invaders. This does raise a difficult question for us now. How much did the British enthusiasm for the truce prove that the German press was right, and the British were simply not taking the war seriously enough – it was not national life or death for them, as it was for the other combatants. Britain had not been invaded. Their national existence was not, so far, at stake. Could we imagine the Argyll and Sutherland Highlanders or the Royal Warwickshire Regiment coming out of their foxholes on the South Downs or on Dover Beach in 1940 to greet the invading Nazis, just because it was Christmas?

There are other uncomfortable questions too. Did the fraternisation let the aggressors off the hook for the slaughter of Belgian civilians, as the Belgian authorities believed? And, even more uncomfortable, did that spirit of unity between fighting men of both sides – which the Christmas Truce became a symbol of – feed into the rise of fascism across Europe? Henry Williamson, one of the participants in 1914, came to believe that one of the people he had met that day Christmas had been Hitler, and it inspired him to join the Blackshirts. He was wrong about meeting Hitler (he refused to take part) but there was a sense, among those who took part, of the unity of fighting men that seems to have delayed the recognition of Hitler for what he was.

On the other hand, the other warring nations have slowly come round to the more relaxed British point of view. When an academic book about the truce was published in France in 2005, the publishers put wrapper around it which called it 'Le Dernier Tabou de 1914'. The first German book on the subject was published in 2003, to enormous publicity.

Seeing the truce through the eyes of those taking part makes it clear that it was never less than patriotic – the British sang patriotic songs, the Germans were driven by their proud sense of ownership over the Christmas festival. But they also saw it as a humanitarian gesture, and an extraordinary one, and one which stayed with those who took part for the rest of their lives – a kind of vision of a world turned upside down.

But there was something else. It was a recognition of a common humanity which had a lasting effect on the people who were there. The realisation that they were fellow human beings in a similar predicament was a passionate discovery. The description of the two sides running towards each other in No Man's Land implies more than a reluctant handshake; it implies a sudden thrilling revelation of how much they had in common. Perhaps in that sense it was, after all, the most important event of the twentieth century, not for anything it was then – though, as we have seen, it moved events along – but for what it tells us about ourselves.

It was an assertion that not all war has to be the same, that it is possible to show some humanity despite the most intense differences. The truce was the subject of a number of pacifist publications, then and now, about the horror of war. But the story may actually demonstrate the opposite: that a just war might still be possible, that not all conflict has to end inevitably in barbarism. If that is so, we must weigh it in the balance against the barbarism that was to come.

The Christmas truce was not political. It wasn't a demonstration or a planned event. But it derived from a fear about what the war had become, and about the competence of the men who led it, and – as such, and paradoxically – it provided a source of inspiration for those who took part. Major Murdoch McKenzie Wood, a Liberal MP who had served with the Gordon Highlanders during the war, rose in the House of Commons in 1930 in a furious speech to explain that he did not fight on the Western Front to kill, but "to prevent killing". He went on to tell the story of his experience of the 1914 truce, shaking hands with his enemies, aware that a "great number of people think we did something that was degrading".

As a result, he said, "I then came to the conclusion that I have held very firmly ever since, that if we had been left to ourselves there would never have been another shot fired."

He may have been right, though it was with the benefit of hindsight. But he was absolutely correct that, for those who took part in the truce, it was a revelation they never forgot.

Acknowledgements and sources

I am enormously grateful to the staff at the Imperial War Museum archive, the British Library, the London Library and the National Archives for their help with this book. I'm also very grateful to my stepfather Robert Crispe, who pointed out a number of mistakes and inconsistencies – though the remaining mistakes are all mine. The truth is that there are hundreds of first-hand accounts now of the Christmas Truce, and more come to light every year. For anyone who wants to do their own research, the following websites are good starting points:

http://www.christmastruce.co.uk/
http://www.1914-1918.net/truce.htm

For anyone who wants to delve a little further into the events described in this book, I can suggest the following:

Malcolm Brown and Shirley Seaton (1994), Christmas Truce: The Western Front December 1914, London: Pan Grand Strategy Series.

Malcolm Brown (2004), *The Imperial War Museum Book of 1914: The men who went to war*, London: Pan Books.

Malcolm Brown (ed.) (2007), *Meetings in No Man's Land: Christmas 1914 and fraternization in the First World War*, London: Constable & Robinson.

Guy Chapman (ed.) (1937), *Vain Glory*, London: Cassell.

Arthur Conan Doyle (1916), *The British Campaign in France and Flanders 1914*, London: Hodder & Stoughton.

Theresa Blom Crocker (2012), *"A remarkable instance": The Christmas truce and its role in the contemporaneous narrative of the First World War*, University of Kentucky thesis.

J. E. Edmonds and G. C. Wynne (1927), *Military Operations: France and Belgium 1915: History of the Great War* Vol 3, London: Macdonald and Co.

Edward Gerald French (1931), *The Life of Field Marshal Sir John French, First Earl of Ypres*. London: Cassell & Co.

Martin Gilbert (1971), *Winston S.Churchill, Vol III: The Challenge of War 1914-1916*, London: Heineman

Andrew Hamilton and Alan Reed (2009), *Meet at Dawn, Unarmed*, Warwick: Dene House.

Maurice Hankey (1961), *The Supreme Command,* Vol 1, London: George Allen and Unwin.

J. P. Harris (2008), *Douglas Haig and the First World* War, Cambridge: CUP.

Max Hastings (2013), *Catastrophe: Europe Goes to War 1914*, London: William Collins.

Lyn Macdonald (1987), *1914*, London: Michael Joseph.

Edward Roe (2004), *Diary of an Old Contemptible: Private Edward Roe, East Lancashire Regiment from Mons to Bagdhad 1914-1919*, (ed.) Peter Downham, Barnsley: Pen & Sword.

Richard Van Emden (2013), *Meeting the Enemy: The human face of the Great War*, London: Bloomsbury.

Stanley Weintraub (2004), *Silent Night: The remarkable Christmas truce of 1914*, London: Simon & Schuster.

Ralph J. Whitehead (2009), *The Other Side of the Wire, Vol 1: With the German XIV Reserve Corps on the Somme, Sept 1914-June 1916*, Solihull: Helion & Co.

Anne Williamson (2004), *Henry Williamson and the First World War*, Stroud: Sutton Publishing.

Henry Williamson (2010), *A Fox Under My Cloak*, London: Faber & Faber.

David Boyle is a co-director of the New Weather Institute, and the author of a number of books about economics, business and the future, as well as history, including *Blondel's Song* and *Toward the Setting Sun*, about the discovery of America. He has written a series of successful titles for Endeavour Press, including *Unseen, Unheard: Submarine E14 and the Dardanelles* and the bestselling *Alan Turing: Unlocking the Enigma*. www.david-boyle.co.uk

Other titles by David Boyle

Building Futures

Funny Money: In search of alternative cash

The Sum of our Discontent

The Tyranny of Numbers

The Money Changers

Authenticity: Brands, Fakes, Spin and the Lust for Real Life

Blondel's Song

Leaves the World to Darkness

Toward the Setting Sun

The New Economics: A Bigger Picture (with Andrew Simms)

Money Matters: Putting the eco into economics

The Wizard

Eminent Corporations (with Andrew Simms)

Voyages of Discovery

The Human Element

On the Eighth Day, God Created Allotments

The Age to Come

Unheard, Unseen: Submarine E14 and the Dardanelles

Broke: Who killed the middle classes?

Alan Turing: Unlocking the Enigma

Rupert Brooke: The Last Patriot

www.david-boyle.co.uk

6903255R00048

Printed in Germany
by Amazon Distribution
GmbH, Leipzig